TECHNOLOGY AT WORK

AT THE
FACTORY

Louise Spilsbury

Raintree
Chicago, Illinois

© 2009 Raintree
Published by Raintree,
a division of Pearson Inc.
Chicago, Illinois
Customer Service 888-363-4266

Visit our website at www.heinemannraintree.com

Designed by Richard Parker and Tinstar Design Ltd
Illustrations by Darren Lingard
Printed and bound in China by CTPS

13 12 11 10 09
10 9 8 7 6 5 4 3 2 1

Library of Congress Cataloging-in-Publication Data
Spilsbury, Louise.
  At the factory / Louise Spilsbury.
      p. cm. -- (Technology at work)
  Includes bibliographical references and index.
  ISBN 978-1-4109-3179-5 (hc)
  1. Automobiles--Design and construction--Juvenile literature. 2. Factories--Juvenile literature. I. Title.
  TL278.S658 2008
  629.2'34--dc22
                            2008005443

Acknowledgments
The publishers would like to thank the following for permission to reproduce photographs: ©A1 Pix p. **9**; ©Alamy pp. **4** (Simon Clay), **5** (Adrian Sherratt), **7** (Trip), **10** (vario images GmbH & Co.KG), **11** (I.Glory), **28 bottom left** (vario images GmbH & Co.KG), **15** (ImageState), **18** (eStock), **27** (Justin Kase zonez); ©Corbis pp. **8**, **28 top right** (Tim Wright), **24** (TWPhoto), **25** (Kevin Fleming); ©Getty Images pp. **6** (Stone/ Michael Rosenfeld), **19** (Johannes Simon), **28 top left** (Stone/ Michael Rosenfeld), **19** (Johannes Simon); ©istockphoto/ VisualField p. **29 left**; ©Wishlist Images p. **29 right**.

Cover photograph of robotic welder, reproduced with permission of ©Getty Images (Photographer's Choice).

Every effort has been made to contact copyright holders of any material reproduced in this book. Any omissions will be rectified in subsequent printings if notice is given to the publishers.

We would like to thank Ian Graham for his invaluable help in the preparation of this book.

Disclaimer
All the internet addresses (URLs) given in this book were valid at time of going to press. However, due to the dynamic nature of the Internet, some addresses may have changed, or sites may have changed or ceased to exist since publication. While the author and publishers regret any inconvenience this may cause readers, no responsibility for any such changes can be accepted by either the author or the publishers. It is recommended that adults supervise children on the Internet.

CONTENTS

Some words are printed in bold, **like this**. You can find out what they mean by looking in the glossary.

INSIDE A FACTORY

A factory is a building where workers make things to sell. In most factories workers have different jobs, but they all help to make the same thing. For example, in a car factory some people make the body of a car, and others put the seats inside. Workers use **machines** to help them work faster and for a longer time without getting tired.

In this factory, cars are made on **assembly lines**. Cars sit on moving platforms that carry them to different machines or people that add different parts.

AT
WORK

PIECES IN A PUZZLE

A car is made from as many as 9,000 individual parts.
It takes between 5 and 30 hours to put the parts together in the factory!

What is a machine?

A machine is a device that makes a **force** greater. Forces are pushes or pulls. For example, you use a knife to eat with because pushing down on the blade makes it easier to cut food into smaller pieces. Using machines means we can do more work with less **effort**. In factories, workers often use **forklifts** to lift weights or loads. They push steel arms underneath the load and push a button or use a handle that raises the arms. Workers using a forklift can carry heavy loads all day long.

Load

Effort

Machines make our work easier or do things we cannot do alone. It would take many people to lift this load without a forklift.

DESIGNING A CAR

The first stage in making any new product is the **design**. Car designers think about who will use the car. For example, a family car needs more seats and space inside than a sports car. Designers consider the size, the shape of the car body, the layout of the inside, the color, and materials to use for seats. Then they make sketches using their ideas.

Using a computer makes it easy to change things like the color, shape, and size of different parts of a design without having to draw the whole car again.

AT WORK

A SLOW PROCESS

Agreeing on the design of a new car can take at least one and a half years! Only then are the new cars made in factories.

Computer modeling and 3D

Designers use computers to make **three-dimensional** (3D) pictures of their design. This is called computer-aided design, or CAD. They draw designs on a **digital tablet**. The tablet senses the push of a pen against it. What designers draw on the digital tablet instantly appears on the computer screen. By using CAD **programs**, designers can rotate the car on the screen so people can look at it from every angle.

Designers sometimes make scale models. These are much smaller models of the final car. This scale model is a quarter of the size of the actual car!

Clay models

Looking at a 3D image of a car on a screen is useful, but often the best way to spot design flaws is to make a model. Design models must be accurate. Some car models are made by hand from foam and are then covered in clay. Others are made by **machines** that follow the CAD design of the car to produce the model.

TESTING THE DESIGN

To find out if a new **design** works correctly, designers create a **prototype**. A prototype is like a real car, with parts that work like a real car. However, it is made slowly by hand and not in a factory.

The strength and safety of a new car design is tested to the limit in a crash test!

INSURANCE INSTITUTE
FOR HIGHWAY SAFETY

CF98018

Safety first

A car prototype goes through different tests to make sure it is strong and safe. In a crash test, workers strap life-size dummies into a car and the car is crashed into a test wall. Testers videotape the test and take measurements to see how well the car protects passengers inside when it crashes. The car design may be adjusted if the tests do not go well.

Wind tunnels

Workers also test a prototype by putting it in a **wind tunnel**. This is a room with a giant fan that blows strong wind at the prototype. The smoother the car, the more easily the air can move around it, and the faster and easier the car can travel. After these tests workers may adjust the prototype's shape so air flows past it more easily.

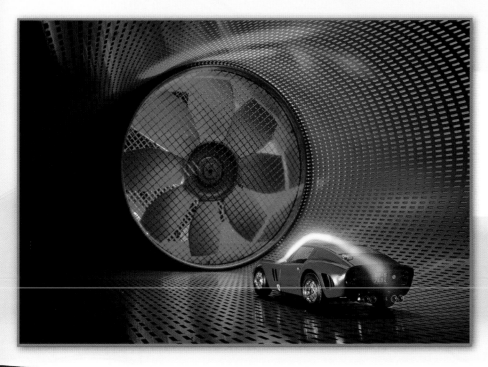

Why do engineers test cars in a wind tunnel like this?

AT WORK

USING LESS FUEL

Wind tunnel tests are important because the harder a car works to drive through air, the more fuel its engine uses. One reason that people want cars that use less fuel is because fuel (gasoline) is expensive.

MAKING A CAR BODY

The car body supports the weight of the car and protects the people traveling inside. It is made from pieces of a tough, strong metal called steel. The steel is delivered by truck or train to the factory in giant rolls. The rolls are flattened, cut, and pressed into pieces of the right size and shape to use for building a car.

Each roll of steel weighs as much as 100 motorcycles.

Cutting steel

Imagine how hard it would be to cut a steel sheet with scissors or bend it by hand into shapes. Workers use **machines** the size of a house to do the work with less **effort**. First, blades cut the flat shapes of the underneath, front end, sides, roof, and doors of the car from steel. Then the shapes are bent into the finished pieces.

In the factory, steel is bent so that it begins to take the shape of the car.

AT WORK

WEDGE

The blade for cutting steel is a strong, sharp **wedge** shape. A wedge is a simple machine. The sharp edge crushes and splits a gap in the metal. Pressing the thin end of the edge in the narrow gap makes the wedge press against the gap, forcing it to open.

PUTTING THE PIECES TOGETHER

The car body pieces are joined together by **welding**. This is when two pieces of metal are heated until they melt together. When the metal cools and hardens you cannot see where the pieces have been joined together. To melt steel, electricity heats metal devices called electrodes. These weld metal parts together at specific spots. That is why this process is called spot welding.

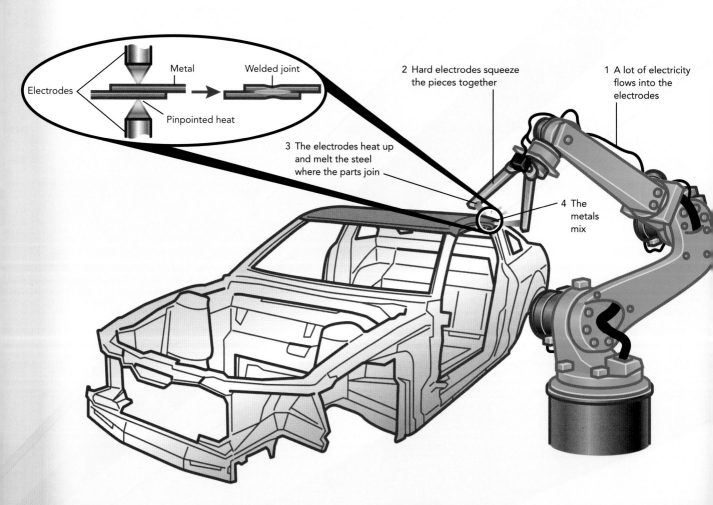

Electrodes

Metal

Welded joint

Pinpointed heat

2 Hard electrodes squeeze the pieces together

1 A lot of electricity flows into the electrodes

3 The electrodes heat up and melt the steel where the parts join

4 The metals mix

ELECTRICITY INTO HEAT

Electrodes heat up because of high resistance. This is when electricity cannot move easily through a material. Electricity is produced by the movement of tiny, invisible particles called electrons. Electrons in the electrode are like a lot of marathon runners moving from a wide street into a narrow alley. They bunch up, jog through the crowded alley, and get hot!

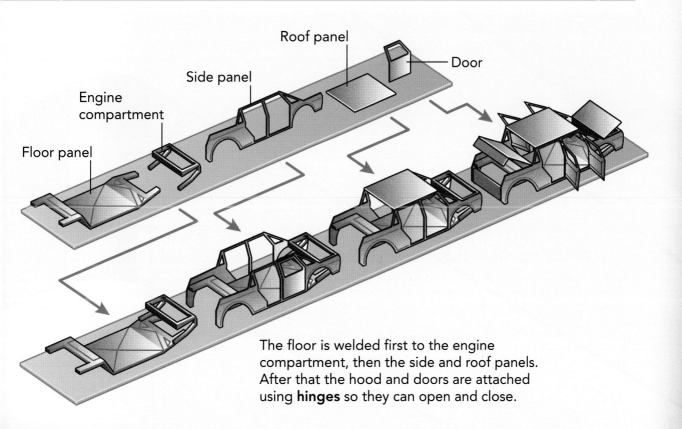

Roof panel

Door

Side panel

Engine
compartment

Floor panel

The floor is welded first to the engine compartment, then the side and roof panels. After that the hood and doors are attached using **hinges** so they can open and close.

AUTOMATIC MACHINES

In many factories, much of the heavy and simple work happens automatically without people. For example, **conveyor belts** move complete car bodies through the factory. A conveyor belt is a belt made of flexible rubber or hard metal plates **hinged** together. A motor makes the belt move along over rollers and carries whatever is on top smoothly along. Sometimes cars rest on stilts on the conveyor belt or on wheeled carts on tracks.

Machine workers

Robots are **machines** that automatically do specific jobs. In a car factory, robots **weld**, paint, and lift heavy items. Factory workers **program** the robots to complete a job.

Robots have some advantages over people as workers. They never get tired, they do exactly the same job each time, they do not need to be paid, and they can do unsafe or dirty work without getting hurt. However, robots are expensive and can only do what they are programmed to do.

IN THE FUTURE

Robots could program teams of other robots in factories and even drive cars!

Most of the welding in a car factory is done by robots! Here you can see a car body moving along the tracks of the conveyor belt.

HOW A ROBOT ARM WORKS

The **robots** in a car factory are really robot arms! Just like our arms, a robot arm is made of different parts that move at joints. However, the parts move using the power of motors rather than muscles.

1. Workers **program** a computer to control how the arm moves.

2. Each joint is powered by an electric motor that allows parts of the arm to rotate toward or away from each other by small amounts.

3. The end piece of the arm carries out the robot's job, such as welding or lifting. It has a **sensor** on it to help it do the job correctly. The sensor also helps people see how well it has been programmed to do the job.

AT WORK

SENSING A ROBOT'S WORK

Sensors are special electronic devices that measure a robot's work and movement. For example, some sensors can tell how tightly a robot hand is gripping and others can tell it how far it is from the next object it needs to work on. This means robot arms can do their job automatically, exactly the same way each time, without being stopped and started by workers.

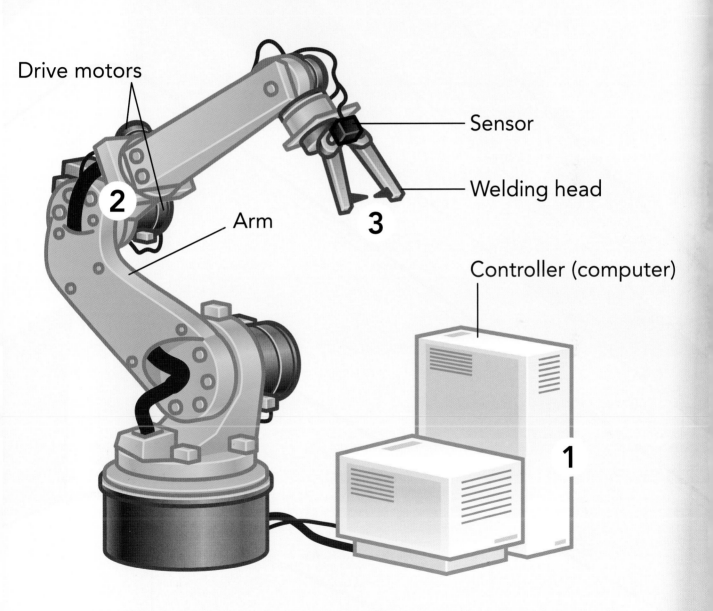

Drive motors

Sensor

Welding head

Arm

Controller (computer)

2

3

1

PAINTING A CAR

The next stage in making a car is painting the body. The unpainted body moves along the **conveyor belt** into the paint shop in the factory. Before being painted, the car is cleaned up. It is dipped in chemicals and sprayed with water to remove any dirt and oil. Then the wet body is blown dry!

Paint is sprayed on using long hoses that are connected to paint storage tanks.

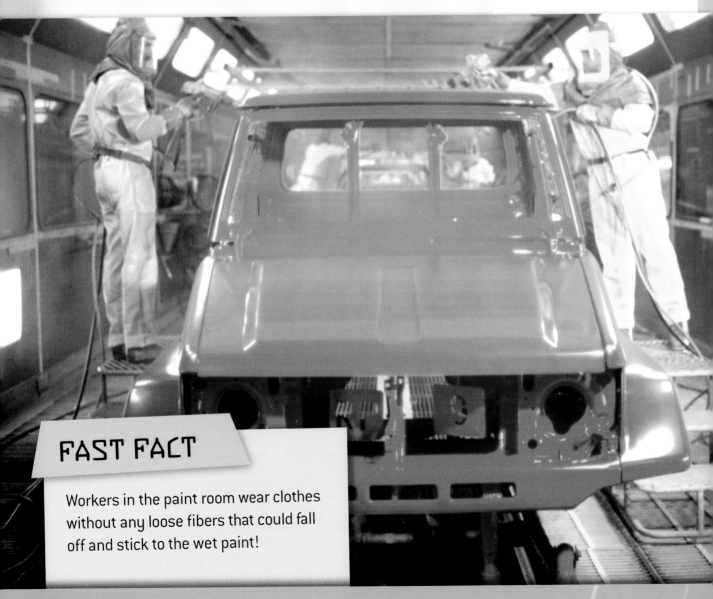

FAST FACT

Workers in the paint room wear clothes without any loose fibers that could fall off and stick to the wet paint!

Three coats

The car body is painted three times. First, it moves into a tank of special paint that keeps the steel from **rusting**. When steel rusts it turns reddish brown and crumbles. This can make a car body weak and unsafe to drive. It also looks ugly. The car then moves into an oven that bakes this special paint so it dries and hardens.

Robot arms like these transform a dull-looking car into a shiny new model.

Next, the car moves past spinning sprayers or **robot** arms fitted with sprayer ends that cover the body evenly with paint. A layer of thick gray paint makes the car surface smooth. The last layer is the final color of the car. Once all the paint is dry, workers glue on pieces that go on the outside of a car, such as the car maker's logo.

VITAL PARTS

A painted car body may look like a car, but is not yet a finished **vehicle**! All vehicles can move in order to transport loads such as passengers and their luggage. The important parts that make a car move, such as its engine, are grouped together in the **drive train**. Workers raise the body above the **conveyor belt** so they can connect the drive train from underneath.

Parts of the drive train

The engine creates power to turn the wheels and drive the car. The steering system and brakes allow the driver to control the direction and speed the car goes. Giant springs between the wheels and the car body provide **suspension**. The springs absorb jolts when the car drives over bumps, so that passengers have a comfortable ride.

AT WORK

STEERING WHEELS

Car steering works by **rack and pinion**. This **machine** changes turning movements into straight movements. The driver turns the large steering wheel. This then turns the narrow steering shaft that twists the pinion. The pinion is a small cog or wheel with grooves or teeth in it. The teeth on the pinion move against teeth on a bar called the rack. Then the rack moves right or left.

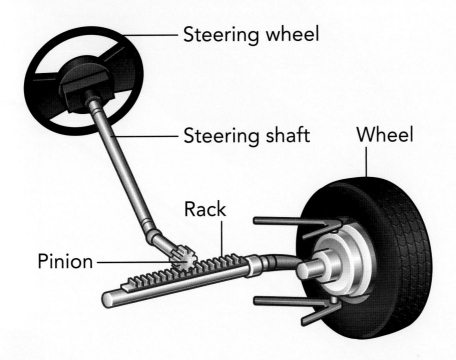

Steering wheel

Steering shaft

Wheel

Rack

Pinion

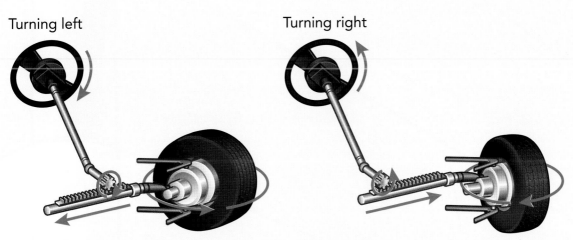

Turning left

Turning right

Turning the steering wheel slides the rack to one side. It pulls the back of the wheel, which turns outward and makes the car turn left.

Turning the steering wheel the other way slides the rack to the other side. It pushes against the back of the wheel, which turns inward and makes the car turn right.

CAR POWER!

A car engine is **designed** to produce power. It looks complicated but is actually a fairly simple **machine**. Most car engines are basically a set of four or eight **cylinders** made of very strong metal. Each cylinder is sealed shut with a sliding plunger called a **piston**. There are openings at the top of each cylinder called valves that can open or close. Fuel burns in the cylinders and causes explosions that push the pistons.

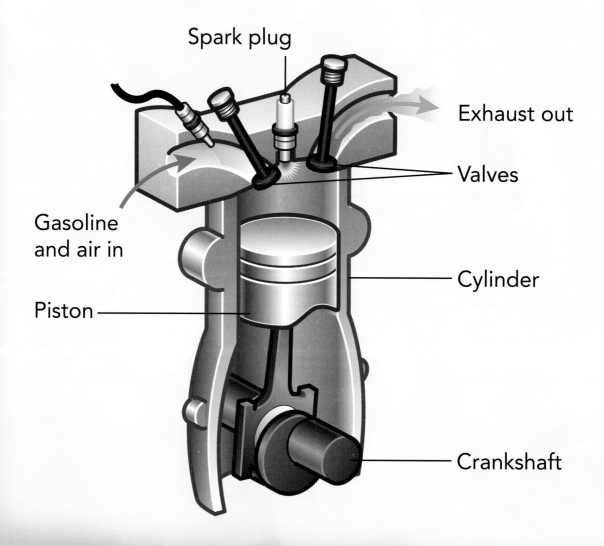

Spark plug

Exhaust out

Valves

Gasoline and air in

Cylinder

Piston

Crankshaft

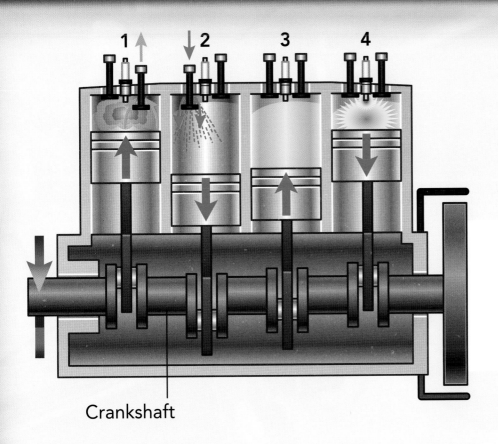

1   2   3   4

Crankshaft

Each piston pushes out in sequence so the crankshaft is spinning the wheels all the time.

The pistons are attached to an **axle** called a **crankshaft** that turns the car's wheels when the pistons push down.

- Gas and air enter the cylinder.

- The spark plug makes a spark that sets fire to the gas and air.

- Gases made by the fire push the piston down.

- The piston makes the crankshaft rotate.

- Waste gases leave the cylinder and go into the exhaust pipe.

IN THE FUTURE

Some experimental cars use hydrogen gas as fuel. Hydrogen burns with oxygen, releasing power and steam instead of dirty exhaust gases.

COMPLETING A CAR

Workers complete a car by adding the final parts. These include the windshield, bumpers, windshield wipers, headlights, and the instrument panel. This plastic panel at the front of a car has instruments such as the speedometer, which shows how fast a car is moving, and the odometer, which shows how far the car has gone. Workers make the car comfortable by adding parts such as carpet and radios.

This worker is attaching the car's instrument panel. An instrument panel is also sometimes called a dashboard.

AT WORK

IN A SPIN

Workers test drive cars to make sure they run and can be driven as they were **designed** to be driven. They drive either on a special track near the factory or by driving over rollers. The spinning tires make the rollers spin the opposite direction at the same speed. The car stays where it is.

Testing

The final stage is to test the completed car. Workers start the car and connect it to a computer. The computer screen shows information from **sensors** in all the electrical parts, such as the lights and brakes. Workers check the information to make sure everything is working correctly.

These shiny new cars are complete and ready to leave the factory.

DELIVERING CARS

Workers do not drive finished cars from the factory to the car dealerships that sell them. Instead, other **vehicles** transport the cars. Some cars are put onto open train cars that stop near the factory. But most cars are put on **auto transport semitrailer** trucks.

1. Many wheels move the semitrailer on several **axles**. Wheels connected to axles are simple **machines**. The powerful force of the engine turns the narrow axle a short distance. This makes the wheel turn with less force, but over the **circumference** of the wide wheel.

2. The wheels are wide, so the load of cars is supported on the ground by the large area of each tire.

3. Several ramps can be raised or lowered to move cars onto higher levels or to stack cars together, so the semitrailer can carry more at the same time!

AT WORK

LETTING LIQUID DO THE WORK

The machines that move the ramps cars drive onto semitrailers are called **hydraulic cylinders**. These are shaped like tubes with **pistons**. Pumps move liquid in or out of cylinders through long narrow pipes. The liquid moves the wide pistons out a short distance with more **force**.

The heavy load of an auto transport semitrailer is supported by wide wheels, which give support on the ground.

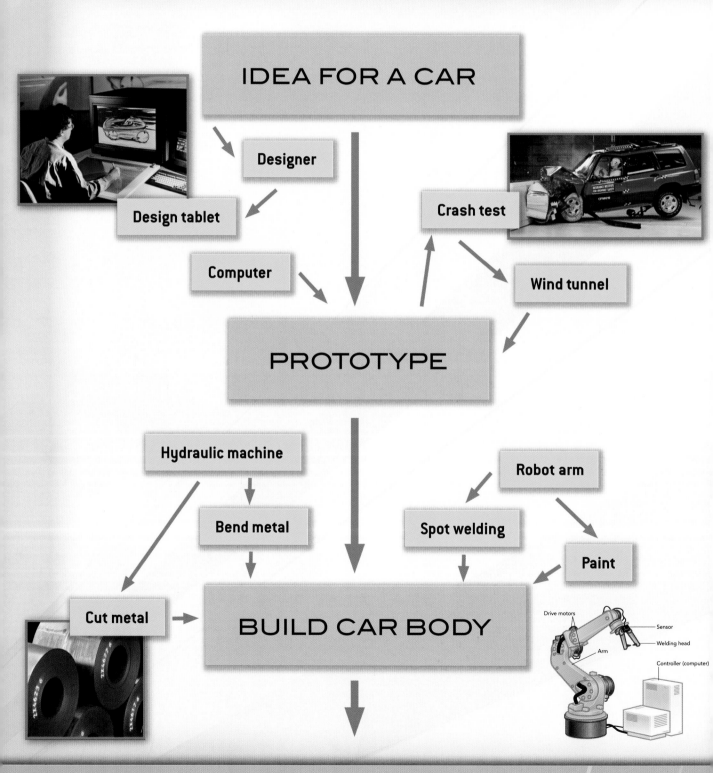

IDEA FOR A CAR

Designer

Design tablet

Computer

Crash test

Wind tunnel

PROTOTYPE

Hydraulic machine

Bend metal

Robot arm

Spot welding

Paint

Cut metal

BUILD CAR BODY

Drive motors

Sensor

Welding head

Arm

Controller (computer)

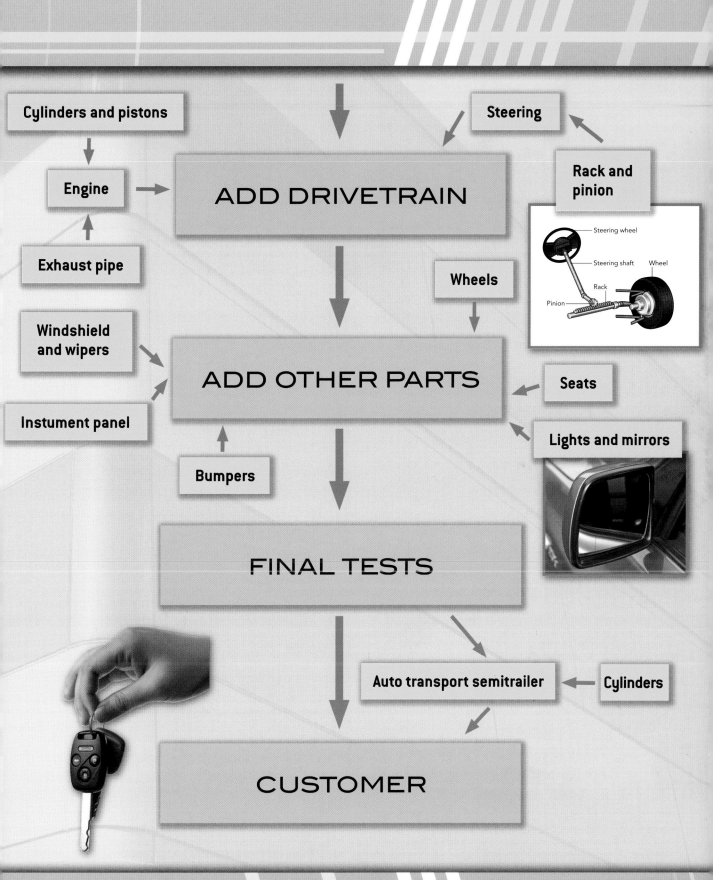

Cylinders and pistons

Steering

Engine

ADD DRIVETRAIN

Rack and pinion

Steering wheel

Steering shaft — Wheel

Rack

Pinion

Exhaust pipe

Windshield and wipers

Wheels

ADD OTHER PARTS

Seats

Instument panel

Lights and mirrors

Bumpers

FINAL TESTS

Auto transport semitrailer

Cylinders

CUSTOMER

GLOSSARY

assembly line system in factories where items being made move between different workers or machines that put together different parts

auto transport semitrailer trailer with many wheels and axles. It holds and transports cars.

axle shaft or rod on which a wheel turns

circumference distance around a circle

conveyor belt moving belt that transports objects. A conveyor belt moves cars through a car factory.

crankshaft rotating shaft in the engine turned by the up-and-down movement of the pistons

cylinder part in an engine where fuel burns to power a car's wheels

design develop a plan for an object, such as a car

digital tablet device a car designer draws on to create an image on a computer

drive train parts that make a car move. For example, the engine rotates the axle and the steering wheel turns the wheels.

effort amount of work needed to complete a task. People use less effort lifting with the help of cranes.

force push or pull making something move

forklift small vehicle used to lift and move loads over short distances

hinge joint that connects two solid objects like a door and a frame. Hinges allow one to swing or move relative to the other.

hydraulic moved using liquid

machine device that helps us do work

piston piece of metal that moves up and down in a cylinder to help turn the crankshaft

program sequence of instructions that computers use to do work. Workers program computers that make robots move and complete a job, such as painting a car.

prototype full-scale working model of a new product, such as a car

rack and pinion set of gears used to change turning force into a straight motion, to steer cars

robot machine that automatically does routine jobs, such as in a factory. People tell robots what to do using computer programs.

rust turn red-brown when steel reacts with oxygen in the presence of water. If cars rust they may get weak and be unsafe to drive.

sensor device that produces an electronic signal when it senses light, distance, or other information

suspension how a vehicle is supported on its wheels. Cars are supported by springs.

three-dimensional something with depth. People can make things look three-dimensional in drawings using shading and shapes.

vehicle machine that transports people or objects. Many vehicles, such as cars, have engines to make them move.

wedge triangular-shaped machine that can be used to split open or cut things

welding join together by heating and melting

wind tunnel room with large fan to blow air over a car or other object

FIND OUT MORE

Books

Abraham, Philip. *Cars (High Interest Books)*. New York: Children's Press, 2004.

Bridgman, Roger. *Robot (Eyewitness Books)*. New York: DK Publishing, 2005.

Parker, Steve. *The Science of Forces: Projects and Experiments with Forces and Machines*. Chicago: Heinemann, 2005.

Sutton, Richard and Elizabeth Baquedano. *Car (Eyewitness Books)*. New York: DK Publishing, 2005.

Websites

www.toyota.co.jp/en/kids/car/index.html
Information about how Toyota cars are made with pictures of the process and inside the factory.

www.greatachievements.org
Sponsored by the National Academy of Engineering, the Great Engineering Achievements website includes a 20th-century timeline of automobiles.

http://teacher.scholastic.com/dirtrep/simple/index.htm
Visit this website to learn more about simple machines.

INDEX